TROY TRAILBLAZER
AND THE HORDE QUEEN

BY ROBERT DEAS

TROY

Space Adventurer.
A reluctant hero
on the surface who
cares more about the
greater good than he
likes to let on.

BLIP

Advanced tactical droid
with a tool for every
job. Likes to spout the
odds of failure, much to
everyone's annoyance.

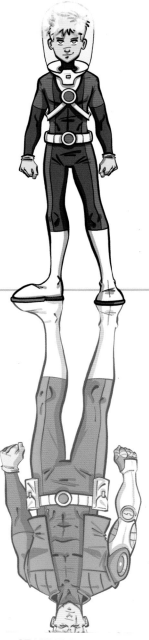

DEDICATED TO
CLAIRE, AMELIE & ISABELLE

Troy Trailblazer and the Horde Queen
is a
DAVID FICKLING BOOK

First published in Great Britain in 2015 by
David Fickling Books,
31 Beaumont Street,
Oxford, OX1 2NP

Text and Illustrations © Robert Deas, 2015

978-1-910200-46-9

1 3 5 7 9 10 8 6 4 2

David Fickling Books supports the Forest Stewardship Council (FSC), the leading international forest certification organisation.
All our titles that are printed on Greenpeace-approved FSC-certified paper carry the FSC logo.

MIX
Paper from
responsible sources
FSC® C020872

DAVID FICKLING BOOKS Reg. No. 8340307

A CIP catalogue record for this book is available from the British Library.

Printed and bound in Great Britain by Polestar Stones.

MEET TEAM TROY

JESS
Former bounty hunter turned good. A fearless and highly skilled fighter.

BARRUS
A furry brute of few words who generally lets his fists do the talking!

THE PATHFINDER

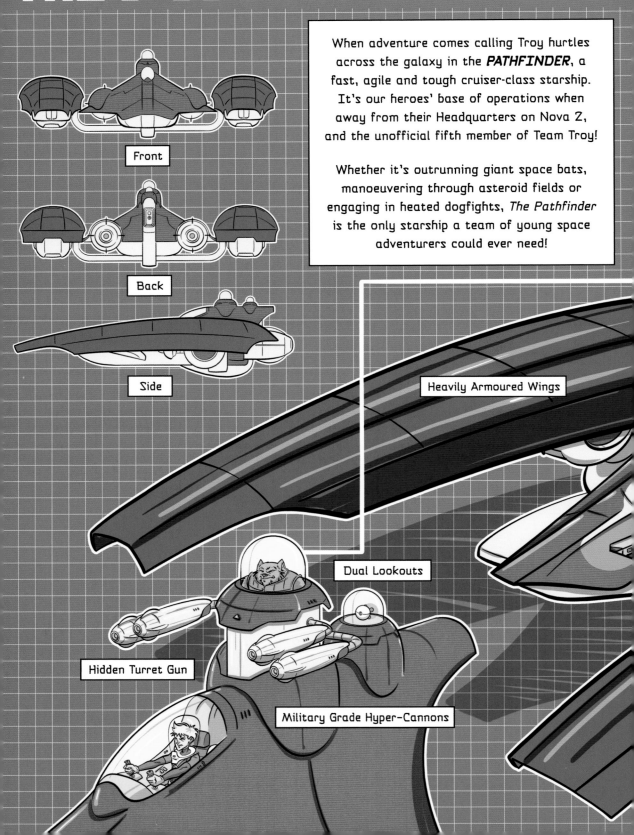

Front

Back

Side

When adventure comes calling Troy hurtles across the galaxy in the *PATHFINDER*, a fast, agile and tough cruiser-class starship. It's our heroes' base of operations when away from their Headquarters on Nova 2, and the unofficial fifth member of Team Troy!

Whether it's outrunning giant space bats, manoeuvering through asteroid fields or engaging in heated dogfights, *The Pathfinder* is the only starship a team of young space adventurers could ever need!

Heavily Armoured Wings

Dual Lookouts

Hidden Turret Gun

Military Grade Hyper-Cannons

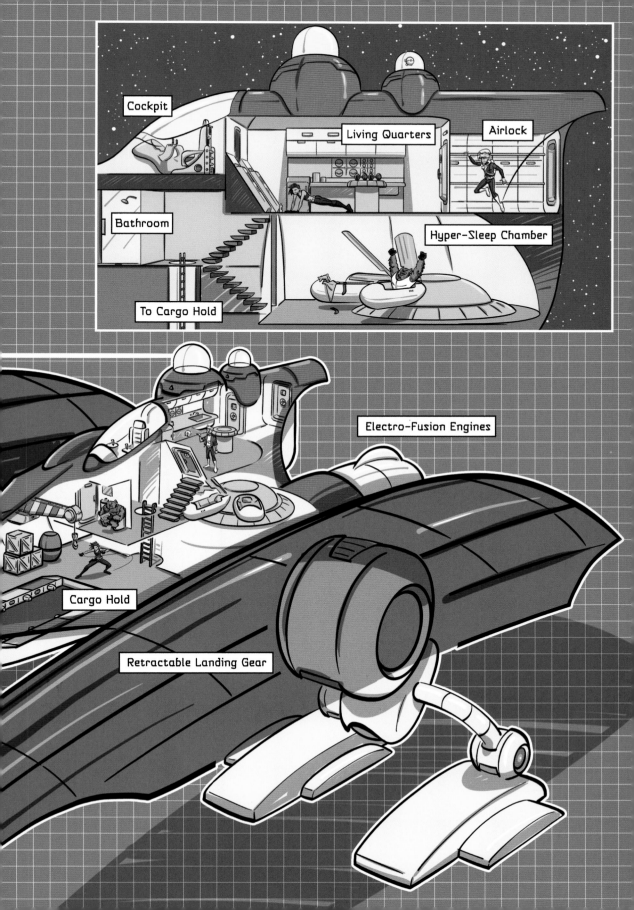

CHAPTER

MISTAKES OF THE PAST

The planet Thargus, the Royal Palace...

STOP!

This is your final warning. Stop or we will open fire!

Grrr, hrmf, grrr, hrff.

Man up, Barrus. It's not like we haven't been shot at before.

That's not something to be proud of, Troy.

P-CHOO

P-CHOO

Grrr!

Argh!

Oomf!

Don't! I have allergies!

RARR!

9

Nice moves, Barrus!

Oh no! *More* guards!

This way, Troy!

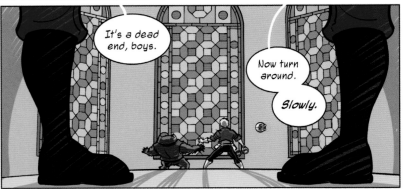

It's a dead end, boys.

Now turn around. *Slowly.*

You really thought you could steal the Infinity Jewel from right under our noses?

You *stole* it first. I'm just taking it back to where it belongs.

You're not *taking* it anywhere.

You've got *nowhere* left to run.

Oh, I dunno...

There's always *somewhere* left to run.

Anyone need a lift?

CLICK

CLICK

Hold it right there, *all of you!* Don't move a muscle.

Sure, you got it.

LAUNCH PATHFINDER

Open fire! Don't let them get away!

P-CHOO

P-CHOO

P-CHOO

Ha ha, why are these guys *always* such terrible shots?

Sorry about the window!

You will be, *boy!*

A little later...

Great job, guys!

Especially you, Jess. You really came through for us back there!

Thanks, Troy.

Hey, you know what we should do?

We should celebrate our first successful mission by hitting the beaches on *Solus*.

I don't really *do* sunshine and beaches, Troy.

Yeah, yeah, we all know *your* idea of fun is starting a brawl in some bounty hunter boozer.

But some of us like to unwind in more conventional ways.

What you call *conventional*, I call *boring*.

It'll be fun, you'll see.

You guys head to the hyper-sleep chamber.

I'll set the autopilot.

AUTOPILOT DESTINATION:

SOLUS

You losers can go to sleep if you like, but I'm going to go *work out* in the cargo hold.

Losers, huh? Come on, let's go bug her.

Grrr!

A little later...

Your working out looks an awful lot like *my* sleeping.

It's called *meditating*, there is a difference.

It helps me keep my edge. You should try it sometime.

That's okay, I'll leave the *honing* my body to be the *perfect weapon* stuff to you.

I can't be there to save you *all* the time, Troy!

Hey, I can *handle* myself and I've always got Barrus as a handy backup if not.

HRMF!

You can be *such* a jerk!

LAUNCH THE DRONES!

Drones? What drones?

Oh...

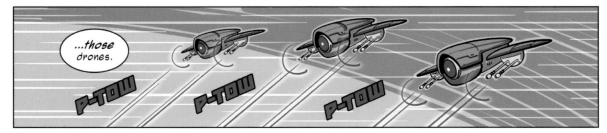

...those drones.

P-TOW   P-TOW   P-TOW

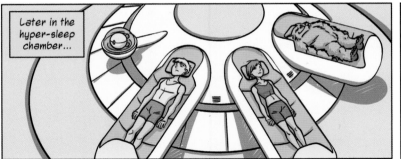

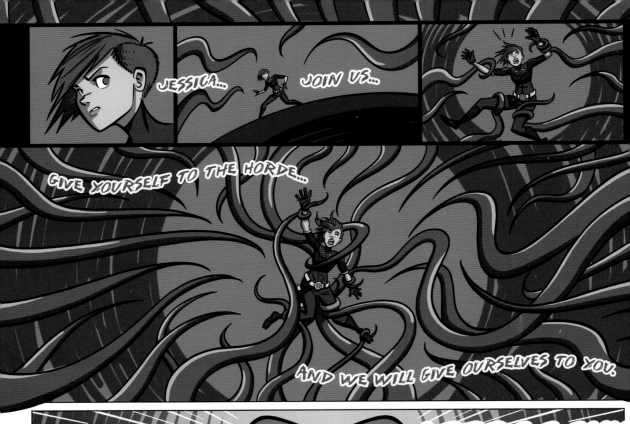

JESSICA... JOIN US...

GIVE YOURSELF TO THE HORDE...

AND WE WILL GIVE OURSELVES TO YOU.

ARRRGGGHH!

Wow. *Intense* dream.

BEEP BEEP BEEP

Huh? Sounds like we're picking up a transmission.

It's a distress signal coming from one of the mines on *Siberas*.

Sorry, Troy.

AUTOPILOT DESTINATION: SIBERAS

The beach is going to have to wait.

Someone needs our help.

25

30

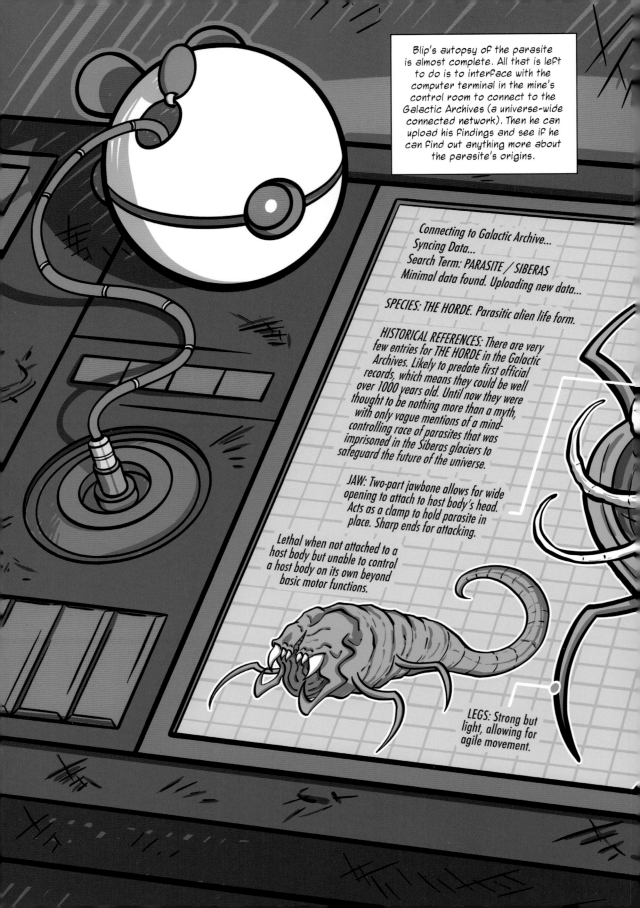

Blip's autopsy of the parasite is almost complete. All that is left to do is to interface with the computer terminal in the mine's control room to connect to the Galactic Archives (a universe-wide connected network). Then he can upload his findings and see if he can find out anything more about the parasite's origins.

Connecting to Galactic Archive...
Syncing Data...
Search Term: PARASITE / SIBERAS
Minimal data found. Uploading new data...

SPECIES: THE HORDE. Parasitic alien life form.

HISTORICAL REFERENCES: There are very few entries for THE HORDE in the Galactic Archives. Likely to predate first official records, which means they could be well over 1000 years old. Until now they were thought to be nothing more than a myth, with only vague mentions of a mind-controlling race of parasites that was imprisoned in the Siberas glaciers to safeguard the future of the universe.

JAW: Two-part jawbone allows for wide opening to attach to host body's head. Acts as a clamp to hold parasite in place. Sharp ends for attacking.

Lethal when not attached to a host body but unable to control a host body on its own beyond basic motor functions.

LEGS: Strong but light, allowing for agile movement.

BLIP'S AUTOPSY REPORT

ORGANIC ELECTRODES: Retractable axons that connect the parasite's brain to the host using suction cups.

BRAIN: Extremely large with incredibly high neural readings. Typical of a hive-mind species to allow telepathic thoughts to be channelled from a queen parasite. It would appear the queen must also be connected to a host to have full control over the smaller parasites and their hosts.

OESOPHAGUS: Extendable, allowing for food to be digested even when attached to the host body.

RIB CAGE: Extremely strong rib bones to protect parasite when attached to host body.

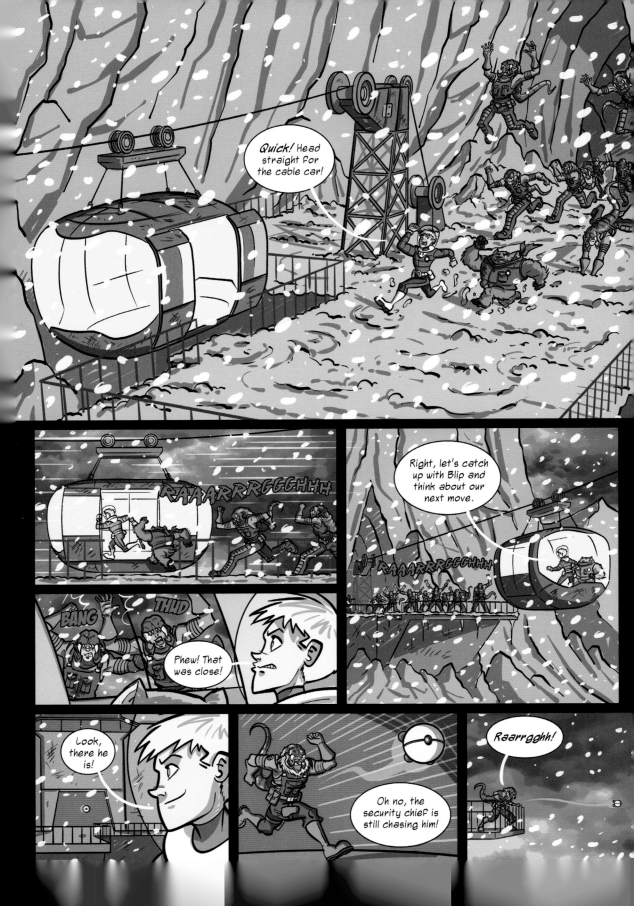

CHAPTER
2

THE FATE OF THE FUTURE

15 YEARS LATER...

After leaving Siberas, the Horde, led by Jess as their queen, swept through the galaxy conquering planet after planet.

A bitter war ensued, but the conflict was very one-sided. The Horde ships dropped millions of spawnling pods that turned their victims into loyal Horde soldiers.

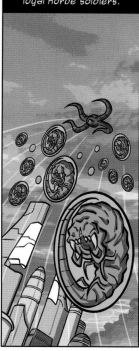

Many planets tried to fight the invading forces, but they were no match for the sheer power and numbers of the Horde.

The final battle is raging on Troy's home planet of Nova 2 and our hero, now the leader of the Horde Resistance, has a plan that may help win the war.

Here they come! Hurry, Barrus! We can't let them catch us!

Quick, in here!

RAAAARRRGGGHHH

I think we lost them.

Now let's head back to HQ. Blip's waiting.

Yeah, *waiting* while we do all the *dangerous* work.

I swear you've got *grumpier* now you can speak.

You'd be grumpy with a voice like mine.

I've told Blip, but apparently he's got more *important* things to deal with.

Which *is* true.

Hey, Blip. We found some transportation. It's a bit of a walk but it's as close as we could get.

Is the cargo good to go?

Almost there.

Just a few final tweaks then I'll be ready.

Okay, I'll keep lookout while you finish up.

Later...

Oh, Jess.

It's gonna be okay. If Blip's as clever as he thinks he is, you'll get her *back*.

A version of me will.

But I'll always be the one who lost her.

Okay, the coast looks clear.

Stick close together. Let's make this quick.

Follow me!

Hey, you run on ahead, Troy. It's not like this is a three-person job!

Grrr, this thing is heavy.

STOP! There's the transport, but it's **surrounded** by Horde soldiers.

Think we're going to need you to play decoy, Barrus.

Grrr! Why can't *you* do it?

Cos you're better at it than I am.

Hey, ugly! Wanna see something cool?

RAAARRRRGGGHH!

See, he's a natural.

Indeed.

A little later...

Huff, huff.

Sounds like the years are catching up with you, Barrus.

You're playing decoy next time. I'm officially on **strike.**

Okay then.

Let's see if Blip's *time machine* works!

Later, as our heroes traverse the war-torn streets...

And you're sure the plan won't work in our time?

I'm positive, Troy. Any action we take against the Queen now will kill Jess too. Their bond is just *too* strong.

So tell me again. How's this going to work?

We'll be travelling back in time to when we first arrived on Siberas all those years ago.

Contact with our past selves must be kept to a *minimum* to avoid unnecessary changes to the timeline. So be stealthy when attaching this *neural overloader* on to Jess.

Remember, you need to detonate it just as the Queen parasite begins to merge with her. The sonic blast should kill off the Horde but leave Jess unharmed.

Sounds simple enough.

What could *possibly* go wrong?

You have an uncanny knack for pre-empting *bad situations*, Troy.

You may want to put your *foot down!*

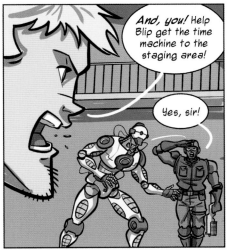

Jess is *here?*

How many times, Barrus? That *isn't* Jess!

Call her that *again* and I'll have Blip deactivate that voice box.

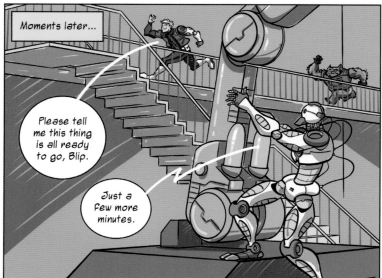

Moments later...

Please tell me this thing is all ready to go, Blip.

Just a few more minutes.

BOOM

It doesn't sound like we've *got* a few more minutes.

Commander, do you copy?

The Horde are in the building, there's *too many* of them!

Give me that radio, soldier.

Hello, Troy.

I know what you're planning. I can read your thoughts like a book.

And I can tell you now.

SCREEEEEE

It's not going to work.

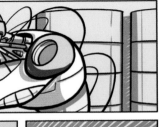